# TIME MANAGEMENT HOW I LEARNED TO NEVER MISS A MEAL

FRANK COPPOLA

# Copyright Notice



**Published by CoppolaCo Publishing**

Published under the Copyright Laws of the Library of Congress of the United States of America by: Frank Coppola,
www.addcoachinggroup.com

**Extraordinaire Graphic Design**
Francisco Jesus Palomo Gil -
Designer and Creative
https://www.domestika.org/it/audente

**Editors**
Diane DeLisa
Kelly Brown

# Limit of Liability

It is a shame in my opinion that I have to include this in my book. I have taken every effort in writing this book to include useful information on the topic of negative self-talk and living a successful life. I do not in any way shape or form guarantee or even imply any level of earnings from anything you might apply from this book or anything else you may purchase or download from me or any of my websites. I cannot vouch for the legality of any of the methods I describe, nor can I be held responsible for any repercussions or reactions that may occur when you apply any of these methods.

All the links that I have included in this book are designed to eliminate the work and effort involved in searching for effective resources with which to build your business, or improve the quality of your life, or to increase and enhance personal growth, and are included with the understanding that to the best of my knowledge, which in some cases may be non-existent, are genuine and reputable sources. However, whenever you make a purchase from one of the websites, links or companies I recommend, suggest or simply compile for your use, I cannot be held responsible for their deliverability or reputation.

Now, my legal notice: This book is designed to provide helpful and useful advice regarding the subject matters covered. However, it is understood that the author and distributor do not engage in the practice of providing legal or professional advice and that the laws and regulations governing the subjects covered in this book may vary from state to state, country to country, and jurisdiction to jurisdiction. It is also understood that the author and any distributors of this book specifically disclaim any liability that is incurred from the use, application, or recommendations of this book. The author and distributors of this book make no representations, warranties, or claims whatsoever regarding the accuracy, effectiveness, legality, or completeness of the information included in this book.

Including but not limited to special, incidental, consequential, accidental, or other damages. As always, legal, professional, tax, accounting, and any other forms of advice should be sought from a professional and is in no way implied in this book. Any and all links and recommendations are for instructional and informational purposes only and are not warranted or guaranteed for accuracy, content, reliability, or reputation, or any other expressed or implied purpose

***The More You Know***
***The More You Grow!***

# Acknowledgements

I want to acknowledge several of my mentors. Their knowledge and insight allowed me to write this book.

First and foremost, David Giwerc, Founder and President of the ADD/ADHD Coaching Academy has taught and inspired me through his example. As a musician, I use the analogy of riffing on this book. I've expanded upon his teachings yet I could not have begun to write this without his coaching, teaching, perspective, diligence and friendship.

I also wish to acknowledge Dr. Fernando Flores. Through the five-year course of study over 20 years ago, he taught me how to think, learn and educate others. His principles are as fresh and original today as they were so many years ago.

To David Neagle who has been a remarkable coach and an invaluable mentor. David has deepened my understanding of Universal Laws. More than anyone, David has made me aware that whatever we want is already within ourselves and we live in an abundant Universe. He's encouraged me and others to live life with dignity, gratitude, grace and faith. All things are possible once we have the desire, make the decision to have what we desire and to get into action.

To all the other people in my life, especially my clients that continue to challenge me to expand and grow; step into your greatness. Your desire to go beyond where you are is courageous and inspirational.

In closing this acknowledgement section, let me know if there is anything I can do to help you increase your personal and professional prosperity and success. The fastest way to reach me is via frank@addcoachingroup. I will contact you within 24 hours and answer any questions you may have.

# TIME

**IS NOT ABOUT**

**SECONDS**

**MINUTES**

**HOURS**

# TIME

**IS ALL ABOUT**

**WHAT MATTERS**

**MOST**

**TO**

**YOU!**

We find ourselves detained, late, and missing from action and repeat offenders of lost time. "I keep missing my appointments." "What do I need to do?" "My wife has given up on me." "What's wrong with me?" "I just bought a fabulous watch." "Where's my watch?"

Still - we're never late for those things that have meaning for us. What matters most gets us to our destination on time: no matter what! Time is always measured by our concerns at the moment.

*Ask yourself, what matters most.*
*Then show up!*

# Introduction

My father owned an Italian Restaurant, C. Frank's Italian Cusine in the Bronx. My entire life was surrounded by "being on time."

When is the store opening? Different days. Different times. What time did we anticipate customers would come? What time would the movie get out? The restaurant was directly across the street from the, a movie theater.

I grew up being very conscious of time.

I am not an expert but I can say I have developed some skills for staying on time.

In the pages that follow, I'll do my best to share some of those skills with the hope you can use them to your benefit.

Enjoy,

Frank

# *TIME MANAGEMENT*
# *How I Learned to Never Miss a Meal!*
## *from the*
## *ADDing Perspective Series for Living*

*Frank Coppola, MA Ed, New York University*
*Founder, Chief Creative Officer*
*International Best Selling Author and Speaker*
*Board Certified ADD/ADHD Coach, ADHD Expert*
*Clarity and Focus Income Accelerator*
*Fearless Entrepreneur Specialist*
*Daniel Amen Brain Health Certification Candidate*
*Clinical Psychotherapist*

Managing time is a consistent challenge for all of us with or without ADD.

What is it about time that has us so puzzled and perplexed? We write down when, where, how and what time we are to be or do or act by such a time and sure enough we are late or completely forget the appointment. It could make you think you have ADD/ADHD

This eBook attempts to give you a new perspective on the meaning of time and ways to handle time. Before we begin, let's take a moment to define ADD/ ADHD. The DSM IV currently uses ADHD, Attention Deficit Hyperactivity Disorder but for our purposes, I prefer the use of ADD/ADHD.

Attention Deficit Hyperactivity Disorder (ADD/ADHD) is a bio-neurological disorder which challenges areas of executive function in this case specifically attention, impulsivity and hyperactivity.

Hyperactivity was considered only physical but most recently, hyperactivity includes cognitive as well. I personally deal with this. I have a very busy mind. I prefer to call this a creative mind.

ADD/ADHD is first and foremost a biological condition. It's chemistry. With proper diagnosis, education and with the aid of an expertly trained ADD/ADHD coach, you learn to see the world differently. Many of my students tell me an understanding of this alone, literally changes their lives . . . forever. I call this **ADDing Perspective** and once discovered and developed, empowerment will take hold.

ADDing Perspective is the ability to recognize what your next action will be, what's expected of you and alike differently.

Please refer to www.addcoachinggroup.com for additional information

# Part 1

## How our brains work

The Prefrontal lobe of the brain is responsible for our executive functions. The executive functions include time, procrastination, organizing, making decisions, attention, hyperactivity, organization and prioritizing to name just a few. In times of stress our bodies produce adrenaline? Adrenaline reduces our capacity to handle these issues effectively. Let's keep this in mind.

## Distinctions of time

In order to have a different relationship with time we need to first determine the distinctions that constitute time. Here is one distinction that you might find interesting.

**There is no such thing as time**. It is not as if Adam turned to Eve and said, "What time to you have? God, told us to be at the tree at 3:30!"

Time is a man-made invention developed as a common ground between us all. Time is social and cultural invention of people delineated by seconds, minutes, hours, months, and years originally based upon the agricultural model. This delineation is essential to our well-being.

## Commitments drive action

Time is an abstract. Many, if not all the time, you might realize that our commitments or what matters to us will have us on time. A commitment is a promise for some action to take place in the future. A commitment is based upon a series of requests and promises with specific agreed upon conditions: conditions of satisfaction at a specific moment. As an ADD/ADHD person I suggest asking several questions before you say yes to a meeting. Ask if you are truly concerned and committed? Are you clear on what needs to be accomplished? Does the meeting matter to you?

Ask what matters and why?

How about being late could get me fired?

## *Get into action*

One of the continuing challenges for us is getting into action. We hang around. We delay. **Procrastination** is one of the challenges that gets in our way.

What drives the action is a commitment: a promise to yourself or someone else. That commitment consistently is based upon something that has you concerned. Relationships, business, going to sporting events, watching the Oscars, seeing a great movie, getting a project completed, picking up your loved ones and so on.

**Do these events truly matter to you?**

With this in the background, if you do not handle time based upon seconds, minutes, hours, etc. but base it upon what matters to you, could you see the possibility of how ADDing Perspective could shift your entire relationship with time?

### *Let's review.*

- Time is man-made.
- Time is social and cultural
- There is no such thing as time.  Really?
- Commitments drive action
- Commitments are based on what matters to you.
- What matters to you is valid and important for ones well-being.
- Opening commitments open new possibilities for being on time.
- ADDing Perspective can shift your entire relationship with time?

# Part II

## Can't vs. Won't

There is a powerful distinction for people with ADD/ADHD namely CAN'T vs. WON'T.  I have found one of the biggest issues for ADDers is the feeling of guilt and shame they experience when they are late, or miss appointments or forget why they came into a room and all the other challenges we face.

Let's go over these distinctions.

Our "unique brain wiring" minds do not function optimally during times of stress; boredom, under stimulation, over stimulation, disinterest, fear, guilt, shame, and excitement (yes). Can you imagine attempting to stay on time under these conditions and how these affect us?

**How can we overcome these feelings that we are responsible?**

One way is to understand the differences between can't and won't.

**Can't is a word that indicates not able.** It's physical. If your brain is under pressure and your body produces adrenaline. When this happens the Prefrontal cortex produces less brain activity. You cannot do exactly what you want to do. Perhaps at these times as much as you desire, you're unable to complete the task. This does not excuse you but it certainly explains the situation.

**Won't is a word that indicates volition.** "No way am I going to take the bus." I choose to not do this." If you do not finish the task or show up on time, clearly you should be held accountable. You might feel guilty, afraid and maybe excited as well. You would need to be responsible for your actions. This is a great opportunity to explore what possibly was in the way. We do this so as to anticipate the possible breakdown in the future. No blame, No shame. No guilt. It's advisable to be in a mood of exploration and wonder.

## Robber Barons of Time

What gets in the way of our commitments and our ability to focus on time management? Education is key to time management. Here are a few of them. Feel free to add anyone that is not listed. I call them the "Robber Barons of Time."

- Interruptions – telephone, personal visitors, meetings
- Indecision - not enough information
- Too much information
- Putting out fires
- Lack of communication
- Blaming others for poor communication
- Procrastination
- Lack of planning

- Boredom
- Stress and fatigue
- Limited boundaries
- Not setting boundaries

## What works and what doesn't work?

The best way to see if time is a challenge is to take inventory.

*Answer yes or no:*

- I'm always late even when I leave enough time. My life is about catching up.
- I have little time for actually planning ahead and sorting out priorities.
- I often find myself caught up with something other than what I was going to do.
- I don't have sufficient time to devote to activities that can increase my well-being and income.
- I'm constantly overwhelmed. I'd appreciate it if someone would bail me out.
- My time is more valuable than my clients.
- I have trouble finding a time management system that works.
- I feel like I'm working overtime but I can't seem to get anything done.
- I overpromise and under-deliver.
- I can't decide what to do.

# Part III
## *Overcoming Time Management Challenges*

OK. Now what?

We need to shift our way of thinking. What is important is to take a moment to envision what we want, how we intend to get it and make a decision to achieve your goal.

For every objective, there is a task or numerous tasks needed to be completed. We also must include a set of goals or markers we can look over at to make sure we are moving to our objective. You may want to investigate a CRM system which can track your progress around a project which invariably is tied to time management.

We are all different. I do not believe in the cookie cutter approach to anything. What works for one person maybe totally different for another. An expert ADD/ADHD coach can be part of your team helping you to discover what approach is most effective for you.

Some of you might be visual while others prefer making lists.

Consider my offer of ***The Double Your Productivity Session*** which will help you discover your strengths to achieve your goal either to start a project or complete a project. You will find this offer at the end of this document. I highly recommend contacting me about taking the offer.

## *Finish strong!*

## *A Few Approaches to Overcome Time Management Challenges*

**Here are a few approaches you can use to handle time. Do you use any of these in your daily life? Do you have others?**

If so, please send them to me at frank@addcoachinggroup.com.

## 1. *Specificity - Get clear on what you want*

Spend a moment to relax. Take 3 deep breaths. Notice how you feel. By stepping back you can view your situation without "needs, should, could ofs" which can cause stress.

Take a moment to write out what you want to accomplish and by what time. This is the one point that keeps derailing staying on track. Codify what you want. Most importantly, write down the "by when." Many people forget this. ***Critical to you staying on time.***

Set up reasonable and measurable goals for without an objective with specific goals in mind, you are a boat lost at sea. Goals keep you directed. Goals mean you matter. They mean you deserve what you want. I make a "commitment list" every morning to figure out my day. Without a goal or objective people tend to just drift personally and professionally. How can you stay on time if you don't know when the project is to complete? Get it?

## 2. *Take time to check your time*

The most important question to ask,

"Is this the best use of my time to achieve my goals. What is the most important use of my time, right now?" This again helps you appreciate how valuable you are to each and everything you desire.

## 3. *What's the plan?*

This is a variation on a boat without a rudder. How can you get where you are going without knowing the end.

Your goal is to create a simple outline. We all know what we want but have no plan for getting there.

In "Think and Grow Rich", Napoleon Hill tells how we all have ideas. What separates the movers and shakers is not the idea. It's the plan.

## *Every idea has value.*

If the idea doesn't become reality, it's always about the plan. When this happens, revise your plan. Successful people make lists constantly. There priorities stay in the foreground. Lists do change, so give yourself permission to bend accordingly.

### *4. Develop an action plan*

The adage comes from carpentry and tailoring: "Measure twice, cut once."

Having an action plan places your goals in perspective. Good enough time management allows you to measure how you're doing. I said, good enough because perfection paralyzes our progress. Keep active and focus on what will make you feel good.

As I mentioned, time management (or self management) is different for everyone. Commitments get you in action. Commitments to what matters to
you, to what feels good in your body as well as your head can assist you with developing the new muscle call time management.

It's all about spending time . . . planning. I prefer to plan with another person or persons as I am a verbal processor getting my ideas through speaking. I can bounce ideas off of them. I know of one person who finds taking a walk gets them focused on their plan.

Another one of my clients gets his best thinking while in motion: the subway, plane, or in a car. Another client uses a rocking chair to develop as well as map out a plan.

Whatever it takes is something you can work with your ADD/ADHD coach who is a dedicated listener to support you in reaching your objectives.

## *5. Set your boundaries from the good opinions of others*

The best way to know your boundaries is learning to say **no**. To know your limits is to be limitless. Saying no gives you time to reach your objectives. By setting your boundary, you give yourself permission and the time to reflect and take action.

## 6. Learn to use a calendar - - - daily

1. Put all due dates and exams in your calendar which is different from a planner.
2. Break assignments into little bits and schedule times to do the assignments whether reading, visualizing, planning and such.
3. Include all your social, work and recreational activities in your calendar.
4. Always have your calendar with you.
5. Allocate 10-15 minutes in the morning or before you go to bed at night to plan your day. This is another critical exercise that can keep you on time.
6. Make a "To Do" list, and keep it in your planner tied to your computer.
7. Make constructive use of your time, e.g., checking on your tasks to reach your objectives and goals.

Time management will most likely continue throughout your life. An ADD/ADHD Coach will work with you to develop systems that can assist you. Your challenge is to use the systems. If you find you can't use them, they are not the right system for you. Work to find one that fits you. Change them if you are bored.

You can work through time management by accepting EVERYONE has time management issues.

Our time management issues overwhelm us under stress. Learn to respect this important part of you; one that can actually support you.

Respect YOUR ADD/ADHD, gather information, seek and accept those people willing to help. We are always learning. Remember it's all good. Your ADD/ADHD coach can help you practice and work through these issues fostering
your independence and success.

### *7. Celebrate and have fun!*

Promise to give yourself a reward for getting tasks completed. You put in the time and rewarding yourself for a job well done is appropriate. It's OK **to give** to yourself and to those around you. The best way to do so is to celebrate, which is an acknowledgement of completion. Learn to balance work and play in the midst of achieving what you desire. You deserve it!

## *Fall in love with your calendar*

***"When you accept your limitations, you become limitless."***

*Frank Coppola*

# 6 Steps to Time Management Mastery Introduction

This is one of the most effective tools for time management and getting work done quickly and effectively.

How many times have you been overwhelmed during the course of your day? You're doing all the "right" things to get you on track. Maybe you have a notebook or several notebooks where you make a list of 20, 30, 50 line items. These items without a doubt you are definitely going to accomplish. By the end of the day you are exhausted and you've barely accomplished 3 or 4 items.

"But I don't understand." The emails are flying. A call comes in and you absolutely must take it which has absolutely nothing to do with what needs to be accomplished. You know, it's a great distraction.

The bid you were going to complete "no matter what" has been forgotten and the job you're working on is delayed. Frustrated, exhausted, annoyed, you tell yourself, "I'll jump on all of this tomorrow. I need to get out of here."

Even worse, you blame everyone and everything as to why you haven't gotten the very things you know you should be doing instead of finding a way to keep you on track, motivated and energized as you knock down and accomplish your goals.

The bonuses for completion could be increased revenue, profits and income. Ah! More money, more time, more peace of mind.

Here is a solution I learned from Chet Holmes, a master salesperson who worked with Charlie Mungers, Warren Buffet's business partner.

Systems bring success because once applied systems reduce your effort. The more systems that work for you, the easier you'll be able to do those things that bring you success . . . ***faster.***

6 Steps to Time Management Mastery has been successful for the likes of Warren Buffet, Richard Branson, Bill Gates and others who must balance a multitude of actions . . . and they do. Granted they have some help. Right?

Still getting into this habit can truly been empowering. I can attest for myself. When I implement the 6 Steps to Time Management Mastery System, I get more done in less time. I've seen my productivity go up a minimum of 40% each time I use the system. Enjoy and good luck!

# 6 Steps to Time Management Mastery System

## STEP 1 - BRAIN DUMP

Gather and capture what you plan to do today by doing a brain dump. The difference is you are going to capture all these thoughts and have them in one place.

## STEP 2: BREAK IT DOWN

Take a piece of 8.5" X 11" paper. Draw a line north and south down the middle of the paper.

On the top of the left hand side write "Things I want to accomplish today". On the right hand side write "Other stuff". You are going to write down all the thoughts, things, must do's down the left hand side. It doesn't matter if you mix personal with business just get your thoughts down on paper. Write down everything.

# STEP 3: JUST 6 and ONLY 6

Choose six (6) and only six (6) things that will give you the highest leverage.

***The highest leverage means those items, activities, things that once accomplished will move you closer to your goal.***

Why just six (6) things? Research has found that though we are processing 60,000 thoughts per minute, we can only accomplish six (6) at a time.

Most likely as you are going back and choosing the six (6) more thoughts will come up for you. Put those thoughts on the right hand side.

One word or a phrase is just as good as any other. The purpose of doing this is to clear the mental clutter that keeps you stuck and to gather your thoughts in one place. Remember this is about getting things done, not about complaining about what you can't get done.

If you put something that pops up that you realize is very important, sway it for one of the 6. Remember. 6 and only 6.

# STEP 4: DO ONLY THOSE THINGS YOU HAVE POWER TO EXECUTE

Now, go back and review the list. Next to those things you want to get done, put a PLUS sign ( + next.)

***Next to those things that you have absolutely no control over put a star (*).***

For the areas that have a star that you have no decision making power . . . cross them off the list. Don't worry about it. It's out of your control. Just move on. Worrying is a great distraction from getting things done and getting what you want.

Go back and look at the things you can do.

Guesstimate how much time each task of the six (6) things that you have chosen will take. If one takes you more than six (6) hours, do not do it. That task is something you would set apart for another day and that is all you would do.

## STEP 5: MY CALENDAR IS MY FRIEND

Now that you have the approximate time each task will take you, place each in your calendar based on time. “Need to get the report in. 1 hour. Put in your calendar let’s say 10 AM. Do this for each of the 6 you’ve chosen.

## STEP 6: THE MORE DIFFICULT, THE MORE REWARDING

Here’s the trick: take the one that is the hardest for you, the one that is the most challenging, the one that you’ll avoid no matter what AND that is the one you do **FIRST.**

Have you ever noticed that if you wait until the end to take the most difficult one you have run out of steam and say “I’ll do it tomorrow”? Doing it first will give you energy. If you cannot complete it within the time you guesstimated, accomplish what you can and move the item to the next day.

### ANSWER EMAILS AT A SPECIFIC TIME

Emails can really eat up your time. Emails can be a tremendous distraction. Set a specific time during the day to answer emails i.e. from 3:30 to 4pm. Lock your door. Announce you’re not to be disturbed.

Get them out of the way.

Time management is a practice. Practice this system and make it a habit.

You can become a master of time but the secret of getting ahead is getting started.

Let's move on to the 60/60/30 Answer and see how to put these steps in action.

# 6 Steps to Time Management Mastery System Review

**STEP 1 – BRAIN DUMP**
**STEP 2 – BREAK IT DOWN**
**STEP 3 – JUST 6 and ONLY 6**
**STEP 4 – DO ONLY THOSE THINGS YOU HAVE POWER TO EXECUTE**
**STEP 5 – MY CALENDAR IS MY FRIEND**
**STEP 6 – THE MORE DIFFICULT – THE MORE REWARDING**

**ANSWER EMAILS AT A SPECIFIC TIME**

***Time management is a practice. Practice this system and make it a habit.***

# The 60/60/30 Answer

Focus - single-minded focus is a challenge I face daily.

# *Focus equals one.*

Whether I'm delaying writing or whether I realize that the "important call" did not take place just drives me crazy.

One of the problems I run into? I'm a multitasker. The problem with multitasking is it doesn't necessarily mean you're going to get the result you want in one area.

**Can you relate?**

I've come across a system that increases focus; single-minded focus. The outcome has been super productive and produces more results. The system fits hand-in-glove with the 6 Steps to Time Management Mastery System and *Get Into Action! 8 Simple Steps to Overcome Procrastination Book*

This technique is enormously effective.

The system is called the 60/60/30 Answer.

Our bodies work on a natural rhythm. We want to get in sync with our rhythm.

# 60/60/30 Answer Relates to Minutes.

### 1. MAKE TIME FOR TIME

First; put everything else on the side for the next two and half hours. Turn off your phone or on mute. Don't answer any emails. Put away anything that can distract you. Why? You will be amazed how much you'll actually get done. Plus, this system allows for very specific breaks. These breaks keep you interested, rested and motivated.

Next it's important you get a hand timer. Using a timer frees you to focus and concentrate on the task at hand. You don't have to be thinking or looking at the clock. You gain so much more than the $29.99 investment.

### 2. PLAN

You can't get to where you want unless you make a plan to get there. Plan what you want to get done into 2 1/2 hours; 2 - 50 minute chunks. In my case I was able to accomplish in 2 1/2 hours what I've been dancing around for over two weeks.

### 3. GET INTO ACTION

Set your timer for 50 minutes. Jump right in. I was surprised how fast the time went by.

When the alarm goes off, take a break for 10 minutes. Set the timer for 10 minutes. Now do anything you want. Change the mood. I did some stretching, deep breathing and walked outside to get some fresh air. Getting away from my desk was like science fiction. You don't realize it but 10 minutes is a long time.

### 4. CHUNK IT DOWN

After your break, chunk on! Set your timer for another 50 minutes - dive into what you want to get accomplished.

### 5. BE AWARE

Whether you are a person living with ADD ADHD or a person dealing with lack of focus and clarity, you may find yourself mentally wandering. This is a great opportunity to learn. Make a note on a separate piece of paper whatever thought you have or had and keep pressing through.

When the alarm goes off it takes another 10 minutes.

### 6. REST, REPLENISH & REFRESH

NOW take a full 30 minute break. Have a small meal. I had a protein drink with blueberries; very refreshing. Completely zone out. Close your eyes and take a 20 minute nap. It will give your mind time to rest, replenish and refresh. You'll find your body can relax and your ability to take on the next task much easier.

The goal is for you to accomplish what you want and increase your self-esteem.

The 60/60/30 Solution will help you gain clarity and keep you focused. Try this once and see if this works for you. I'd love to hear from you and how you might use 6 Steps to Time Management Mastery.

Contact me at frank@addcoachinggroup.com
frankcoppola01@gmail.com

## 7. *Celebrate and have fun!*

Promise to give yourself a reward for getting tasks completed. You put in the time and rewarding yourself for a job well done is appropriate. It's OK **to give** to yourself and to those around you. The best way to do so is to celebrate, which is an acknowledgement of completion. Learn to balance work and play in the midst of achieving what you desire. You deserve it!

Time to get into action!

Thank you for taking the time to review ***TIME MANAGEMENT – How I Learned to Never Miss A Meal.***

***Double Your Productivity Session*** is a free 1:1 session with me. This call is a 45 minute deep dive working on your unique situation.

We will:

1. Focus on your vision
2. Isolate challenges, blocks or areas where you are being held back to reach your goals and how best to clear them up.
3. Discover your power for success.
4. Set a game plan over the next 90 days to reach them.

***The Double Your Productivity Session*** is special. You get to be with me 1:1 for 45 minutes which is valued at $750 per hour. I promise you, you will walk away with possibilities you haven't imagined.

When you take advantage of Double Your Productivity Session you will receive a bonus for doing so,

I look forward to hearing from you.

***In gratitude,***
***Frank, March, 2022***

# RESOURCES:


Special thanks to David Giwerc, MCC, ADD Coaching Academy, www.addca.com

Coppola, F. (2011) 6 Steps to Time Management Mastery., New York, NY: Frank Coppola, CoppolaCo Media

Dr. Fernando Flores, http://www.centipedia.com/articles/Fernando_Flores

Hallowell, E. & Ratey, J. (1994). Driven to Distraction. New York: Pantheon Books.

Hallowell, E. & Ratey, J. (1994). Answers to Distraction. New York: Pantheon

Coppola, F. (2005). "10 Ways to Benefit with ADD – Transforming the ADD/ADHD Conversation"

Hartmann, T. (1995).--------. Underwood Books.

Kelly, K. & Ramundo, P. (1993). You Mean I'm Not Lazy, Stupid or Crazy? Cincinnati, Ohio: Tyrell & Jerem Press.

Tufts University. http://www.tufts.edu/hr/tips/time.html

Uncle Max Says.com

Weiss, L. (1992). Attention Deficit Disorder in Adults. Dallas, TX: Taylor Publishing Company.

Coppola, F. (2011) Get Into Action – 8 Powerful Steps to Overcome Procrastination and Overwhelm

Weiss, L. (1994). Attention Deficit Disorder in Adults Workbook. Dallas, TX: Taylor Publishing Company

# ABOUT THE AUTHOR

## *Who Is Frank Coppola?*

***"Once you align your business around your strengths and tap
into your inner brilliance you can begin to experience a fast and dramatic increase in the flow of money and success."***

***By using the "Natural Learning State" my client's consistently
get more done and enjoy greater clarity (freedom), focus (speed)
and profits (success).***

Frank Coppola is a transformational coach and mentor who helps entrepreneurs, business owners, health professionals; (out-of-the-box thinkers, non-conformists and creatives) identify their strengths and talents and utilize them to create successful business and life - ***faster.***

Even if plagued with overwhelm; procrastination and a string of unfinished projects Frank works with clients to discover their natural strengths, uncover hidden talents and leverage them to create business that supports big ideas and passions.

Frank is an authority in discovering how to turn your creativity into the most powerful and profitable asset you have, giving you the power to create all of the money, success and freedom you want! His clients are delightfully surprised at how fast they are able to exceed their own income goals and consistently grow their businesses. It is not unusual for clients to double their income in less than 6 months.

Frank has been the go-to ADHD specialist. He's coached clients of international brain authorities like Dr. Daniel Amen and others.

Frank's 25 years as an entrepreneur in the creative arts and as a singer/ songwriter for himself and for talent such as the legendary Temptations, Whitney Houston and other musical superstars gives him unique insights on how to harness creativity and make it work for you.

Recently, Frank created the signature song ***You're More Than Enough*** for Eiji Morishita's ***Speak Your Genius*** Event.

Most recently he was commissioned to write ***We Rise Again: A Video & Music Tribute to 9-11...and YOU.***
*https://www.youtube.com/watch?v=P2ylfjOMKc0*

WE RISE AGAIN is dedicated to all the fallen heroes, first responders and all those affected by the tragedy of 9/11 and to those who struggle, now and forever.

Other clients include: Ford, AT&T, MTV, Chase, IBM, Coca-Cola, SNL, Volkswagen and Johnson & Johnson and showcase how diverse his business expertise is.

*Frank Coppola, MA Ed, New York University*
*Founder, Chief Creative Officer*

*International Best Selling Author and Speaker*
*Board Certified ADD/ADHD Coach, ADHD Expert*
*Daniel Amen Brain Health Certification Candidate*
*Clarity and Focus Income Accelerator*
*Fearless Entrepreneur Specialist*
*David Neagle Certified Miracle of Money Coach/Mentor*
*Executive Business Consultant*
*Sales Results Expert, Chet Holmes*
*Ontological Designer (Organizational Design) Dr. Fernando Flores*
*International Motivational & Inspirational Singer/Songwriter*

## TESTIMONIALS

*I've had the pleasure to work with Frank over the past several years. Frank has been a client of mine and knows as much as anyone out there on how to identify your talents and strengths and utilize them to create successful business - faster. Amongst his unique talents are the ability to create music that reinforces and deepens core business strategies and Universal Principles we all need to become ultra-successful. Frank's music and voice touches on a soul and cellular level in a way that few people in our industry can achieve. Take a moment to experience his unique approach. I highly recommend it.*

**David Neagle-Master**
**Income Accelerator**
**& Mentor for**
**Entrepreneurs & Corporate Professionals**
**www.davidneagle.com**

*"Using Frank's expert guidance, I took a stalled project from $0 to over $121,465*
*in less than 12 weeks!"*

**Stephanie Frank – The Accidental Millionaire**
**www.stephaniefrank.com**

*"I made a quantum leap coaching with Frank in all areas of my life.*
*I made as much money in 5 months than I did all of last year"*

**Bob Kopp -Financial Advisor**

*"I had difficulty focusing. My business was flat because I was so scattered.*
*I started working with Frank. After 3 weeks, I made $32, 768. Holy Crap!*
*What I am truly grateful for is his ability to help me articulate all of me.*

***Gerald Franconi - Designer,***
***Artist, Visionary***

*Frank Coppola is one of those people who are able to make you reflect on how you should lead your life. You have to know him, in order to understand that his experience and professionalism have an added value:*

*"It is  the key for your business and life to succeed."But Frank has another special charm. He is a wonderful person, from beginning to end, he is a professional in dealing with people, and he can help you be happy in your working life, something that today is not so easy to achieve.*

*He is going to help you be a better person and entrepreneur.*

*That is why he who knows him is already em[pwered. you can no longer go without him.*
*I thank God for finding you on the path of my life.*

***Francisco Jesus Palomo Gil - Designer and Creative***
***https://www.domestika.org/it/audente***

*Frank's coaching & mentoring approach is simple and direct. His book is chock full of great advice for the ADD ADHD challenged person, which means everyone. For everybody who struggles to turn their dreams into reality, Frank Coppola's book shows the way."*

***- Dr. James Canton, Futurist***
***Institute for Global Futures***

*"When I met Frank I told him I had so many ideas I didn't know what to do next and where to focus. My business and cash flow were suffering. Within four weeks of working with Frank, I've generated $42, 690.*

***Marcus Thomas –Entrepreneur***

*When I met Frank I was struggling to get a job.  He guided me through a series of surveys to uncover my hidden talents and strengths as well as exercised that focused on what I truly loved to do. Frank kept on telling me to be clear on what I wanted.  There is a job there for me.  He gave me hope.*

*Within 3 weeks I had 4 job interviews and within a month, I was offered a job as Manager, Creative Strategy for Lead Dog - an environmental advertising agency.*

*My dream job.Thank you, Frank.  Thank you.*

***Zach Solomon Manager: Creative Strategy***
***Lead Dog Agency***

**Frank's proven solution for turning procrastination into your greatest advantage is sheer genius!** We thoroughly enjoyed having him as one of our
***Virtual World Peace Gathering guest speakers.***

*Frank Coppola's song* ***One World One Love,*** *which is available on iTunes, is a great example of his artistic creativity. He is a master at helping people who work long, hard hours and still struggle to make money and show a profit.*

***~ Terry Earthwind Nichols & Linda Vettrus-Nichols Chairman, Evolutionary Healer, LLC; Ambassador at URGC - Global on Refugees; Poet, Int'l Speaker; Father of Repetitive Behavior Cellular Regression™; Contributor to Good Men Project***

## *MUSIC*

**WE RISE AGAIN - A VIDEO & MUSIC TRIBUTE to 9/11 ... and YOU!** https://youtu.be/P2ylfjOMKc0

*WE RISE AGAIN is dedicated to all the fallen heroes, first responders and all those affected by the tragedy of 9/11 and to those who struggle, now and forever.*

Please pass this along pass this inspirational video along to family, friends, associates, kind hearts and others if this resonates with you.

Goal: 1 Million people hear the song before next 9/11 in honor of my cousin, first responders, others who died and all the families.

Why did I write and perform the **WE RISE AGAIN**? I lost my cousin John Sherry as well as 23 people I personally knew from Cantor Fitzgerald.

Since the video and song were released last Friday, September 10, 2021, it's reached 28 countries including Japan, China, Viet Nam, Spain, Portugal, Ireland, Russia, Belgium, France, Italy and Brazil throughout the United States and Canada by people sharing. Please join in.

***CD***

*Coppola & Rosengarten - One World One Love – A Celebration of the Human Spirit*

***BOOKS***

*TRANSFORMING THE ADD CONVERSATION – 10 Ways to Make It Happen*

*GET INTO ACTION – 8 Powerful and Simple Steps to Overcome Procrastination and Overwhelm*

*TIME MANAGEMENT – How I Learned to Never Miss a Meal*

*HIGH PERFORMANCE ADD/ADHD - Success Stories from 12 Influential Figures Who Prospered & Succeeded With ADD.*

## *OTHER YOUTUBE SONGS*

*OneWorldOneLove*
*https://www.youtube.com/results?search_query=one+world+one+love+coppola%2Frosengarten*

*Turn it over - https://www.youtube.com/watch?v=MQ0aZc4885M*

***You deserve to be happy, prosperous & successful doing exactly what you love to do***

ADD Coaching Group - 514 West End Avenue - New York, New York 10024
www.addcoachinggroup.com frank@addcoachinggroup.com
V. (646) 295-5625 F. (212)-579-0270
The ADD Coaching Group is a
Division of Edutainment, Inc.

Made in the USA
Monee, IL
04 November 2026

67377388R00020